The Irish Kitchen

Breads & Baking

The Irish Kitchen Breads & Baking

Ruth Isabel Ross

Gill & Macmillan

Gill & Macmillan Ltd
Hume Avenue, Park West
Dublin 12
with associated companies throughout the world
www.gillmacmillan.ie
© Ruth Isabel Ross 1995, 2003, 2007
978 07171 4242 2
First published in this format 2007

Index compiled by Helen Litton
Illustrations by Eva Byrne
Design by Slick Fish Design
Print origination by Carole Lynch
Printed in Malaysia

This book is typeset in 9/14 pt Avenir.

A catalogue record for this book is available
from the British Library.

1 3 5 4 2

Contents

Glossary of Equivalent Terms

Irish Term	US Term
biscuit	cookie
cling film	plastic wrap
loaf tin	loaf pan
mixed spice	allspice
prove/proving	proof/proofing
'rubbing butter into flour'	'cutting butter into flour'
sultanas	yellow raisins (dried green grapes)

Conversion Table

Imperial	US	International (Metric)
1 tsp	1¼ tsp	6 ml
1 tbsp = 3 tsp	1¼ tbsp	18 ml
1 cup = 10 oz	1¼ cups = 10 oz	296 ml
1 pt = 2 cups, 20 oz	1¼ pt = 2½ cups, 20 oz	591 ml

US	Imperial	International (Metric)
1 tsp	¾ tsp	5 ml
1 tbsp = 3 tsp	¾ tbsp	15 ml
1 cup = 8 oz	¾ cup	237 ml (approx ¼ L)
1 pt = 2 cups, 16 oz	⅘ pt = 1⅔ cups, 16 oz	473 ml (approx ½ L)

Introduction

Visitors to Ireland go home with glowing accounts of Irish baking. They enthuse especially over Irish bread. Sustaining, usually dark brown and available in every first-class restaurant, it is delicious with fresh butter, with smoked salmon — with almost anything. Luckily it has been confirmed lately that good bread is healthy, body-building for children and fortifying for adults.

This rough brown bread has been made in Irish homes for hundreds of years — the tradition has never lapsed from the time when people lived too far from towns to go to

bakeries. In cottages and small farmhouses, bread, fruit loaves and cakes were made in a skillet or pot oven over an open hearth. The skillet swung over the turf fire on a homemade crane. There was an open fire below the skillet, and burning embers were shovelled on top of the lid to make the bread cook from above as well as below.

Though small houses were limited to hearth cooking, the 'big house' and the larger farmhouses boasted wall ovens and solid fuel ranges. Every kind of baking could be done in these — yeast breads, pies, puddings, cakes and biscuits. Rough brown bread was also popular in the finer houses and was made each day. Every house in the Irish country-side was, and sometimes still is, pervaded by the whole-some smell of baking bread.

The recipes in this collection start with several for soda or country bread, simple to make using white or wholemeal/whole-wheat flour. These are followed by some for yeast bread, more complicated than country bread, lighter in texture, delicious and easier to digest. People who can make yeast bread are much admired. They have a talent that goes to the heart of skilful cooking and can recognise the warm, pleasant feel of the kneaded dough when it is ready for proving.

The Barm Brack, or fruit bread made with yeast, has a special tradition in Irish life. It was eaten on New Year's Eve and on the feast of St Brigid on 1 February. But Barm

Brack was specially known in the Hallowe'en jollifications when a ring would be put in the mixture — whoever found the ring in his or her slice would be married within the year. This caused jokes all round.

Among the recipes in this book are some mixing flour with potato, like the one for soft pastry on page 44. This has always been popular in Ireland, as are the well-known potato cakes, eaten with melting butter. Boxty pancakes made with grated raw potato (pages 42–3) are tradition-ally served on All Saints' Day and very satisfying they are.

Cakes were sometimes baked in a pot oven. Most were not iced, but were often enriched by spirits or stout and served on special occasions. Each housewife had her own specially guarded recipes to be passed on only to daugh-ters, grand-daughters and intimate friends.

The cake recipes are mostly simple to make, so are adapt-able for modern life and tastes. The biscuits are the same. Both are mixed much more easily by the melting method whereby butter, syrup and sugar are warmed and poured onto the flour mixture. This method is introduced in many of the traditional recipes here.

Savoury pies slowly became popular in Ireland, probably as a way of keeping meat warm and moist. The meat also went further, making pies economical. Pastry recipes were adapted from abroad many years ago and became part of the Irish diet, like steak and kidney and chicken pies.

Donegal and Dingle pies (pages 67 and 68) have become local dishes.

The last section in this book is for simple 'no flour bakes'. Is this a contradiction in terms? Surely not. We all like light food sometimes. Some people are avid slimmers, a few are allergic to flour. With or without flour, we can all enjoy the concentration of flavour, the nourishment, the sheer convenience that baking gives to almost any food.

Country Breads

Brown Soda Bread
White Soda Bread
Nutty Brown Bread
Tea Bread
Irish Treacle Bread
Oaten Loaf
Rough Brown Bread
Sally Lunn Teacake
Griddle Bread

When people write or talk about Irish country bread, they mean bread made without yeast, leavened by bread/baking soda or baking powder. It is the most loved of our traditional breads and its solid nourishment gives more pleasure than almost any Irish food. It also gives us a feeling of continuity with the past. The Irish have never stopped making soda bread at home.

Our earlier bread was often made with oats and not with wheaten flour. The oaten loaf in this section is a modern version of oaten bread. It is rough and primitive, hard on the digestion, but it has something for modern tastes as it includes bran. It is like a flat, nutty brick.

It is doubtful if anything was weighed much in the old days. People just didn't have time. They threw handfuls of flour and oatmeal of different sorts into a bowl and mixed them with buttermilk. When the texture felt right, the dough was crossed deeply and bundled into a hot oven or cooking pot. Forty minutes later, it had become a loaf which was robust and individual. Some people put herbs into their bread and very good it tasted.

No loaf tins are needed for country bread. It bakes far better when placed straight onto a floured baking sheet in a strong and steady oven. There must be a wire rack and a clean tea towel/dish cloth ready to wrap the loaf in when it is baked.

BROWN SODA BREAD

This is the classic Irish recipe for brown soda bread.

- 125 g/4 oz/1 cup white (all-purpose) flour
- 350 g/12 oz/3 cups coarse brown (whole-wheat) flour
- 1¼ tsp/1½ US tsp bread (baking) soda
- 1 tsp/1¼ US tsp salt
- 250 ml/9 oz/1¼ cups buttermilk (approximately)

Mix all the dry ingredients in a large mixing bowl. Make a well in the centre and add the buttermilk gradually, using a knife to mix. As soon as a dough is formed, turn it onto a floured board and knead it lightly. It should become soft and elastic. Form a round loaf. Prick it with a fork and cut a deep cross in the top of the loaf. Place on a baking sheet and bake at 200°C/400°F/gas 6 for 35 minutes. The loaf should sound hollow, top and bottom, when fully cooked. Wrap the loaf immediately in a clean tea towel/dish cloth and put it on a rack to cool.

WHITE SODA BREAD

A simple but popular bread, especially good with home-made blackcurrant jam.

- 450 g/1 lb/4 cups white (all-purpose) flour
- ½ tsp/generous ½ US tsp bread (baking) soda
- ½ tsp/generous ½ US tsp salt
- 280 ml/½ pint/1¼ cups buttermilk (approximately)

Sieve/sift the flour, salt and bread/baking soda into a bowl. Make a well in the centre. Pour in most of the buttermilk to make a loose dough, adding more if necessary. Turn the dough onto a floured board and knead it very slightly. Turn the smooth side up. Flatten it carefully and cut a deep cross on the top. Bake at 200°C/400°F/gas 6 for about ¾ hour or until the loaf sounds hollow if you tap the base. (You may need to turn it over for 5 minutes or so to achieve this.) Place the loaf on a wire rack with a clean tea towel/dish cloth over it to let it cool slowly.

NUTTY BROWN BREAD

This bread is dark brown and has a 'gritty' texture.

- 50 g/2 oz/½ cup pinhead oatmeal*
- 175 g/6 oz/1½ cups wheatenmeal (whole-wheat) flour
- 75 g/3 oz/¾ cup white (all-purpose) flour
- ½ tsp/generous ½ US tsp sugar
- 1 heaped tsp/1¼ US tsp bread (baking) soda
- 280 ml/½ pint/1¼ cups buttermilk

Put the oatmeal, flours, sugar and bread/baking soda into a bowl and sift with your fingers. Add the buttermilk. Mix everything with a wooden spoon. Knead slightly. Place the dough in a greased tin and bake at 200°C/400°F/gas 6 for 30–35 minutes.

Wrap the loaf in a clean tea towel/dish cloth to keep it from becoming hard. Do not cut it for a few hours but finish within 24 hours.

Sometimes called Irish or Scottish oatmeal, these steel-cut oats have a nutty texture.

TEA BREAD

A light tea bread, less solid than ordinary white soda bread, it is both crumbly and sweet.

- 350 g/12 oz/3 cups self-raising flour
- 1 level tsp/1 generous US tsp salt
- 75 g/3 oz/¼ stick margarine
- 50 g/2 oz/ 2 US tbsp sugar
- 1 egg, beaten
- 200 ml/7 oz/ ⅔ cup milk

Combine the flour and salt, then rub in the margarine. Add sugar and mix to a light dough by adding the beaten egg, then the milk. Knead lightly on a floured board. When the dough is elastic, form it into a loaf. Prick it well with a fork. Bake at 200°C/400°F/gas 6 for 30–35 minutes.

IRISH TREACLE BREAD

A rich-tasting bread that keeps well and needs fresh butter.
Treacle bread can be made more interesting with a tablespoon
of grated orange peel or some ginger added to the mixture.

- 450 g/1 lb/4 cups white (all-purpose) flour
- 1 level tsp/1¼ US tsp bread (baking) soda
- 1 level tsp/1¼ US tsp baking powder
- 50 g/2 oz/2 US tbsp sugar
- 75 g/3 oz/¾ stick butter
- 2 tbsp/2½ US tbsp black treacle (molasses)
- enough buttermilk to make a stiff dough (a little more
  than 280 ml/2 pint/1¼ cups)

Sift the dry ingredients into a bowl. Melt the butter with the
treacle/molasses and add it to the flour mixture. Mix these
well with a wooden spoon. Mix in enough buttermilk to
make a firm dough. Knead this a little.

Roll the dough to 5 cm/2" thick. Make 4 'farls' or quarters by cutting a cross in the top. Bake in centre of oven at 200°C/400°F/gas 6 for about 40 minutes. Tap the loaf for a hollow sound. When it is done, put it on a wire rack and cover with a clean cloth.

OATEN LOAF

A modern version of the primitive loaves which were made before wheat was easy to find. This solid loaf will keep well.

- 175 g/6 oz/1½ cups oatmeal
- 175 g/6 oz/1½ cups pinhead oatmeal*
- 140 g/4½ oz/1¼ cups oat bran
- 1 tsp/1¼ US tsp baking powder
- 1 tsp/1¼ US tsp bread (baking) soda
- 1 tsp/1¼ US tsp brown sugar
- 1 tsp/1¼ US tsp salt
- 600 ml/1 pint/2½ cups buttermilk

The instructions are simple. Mix everything together in a bowl and leave to stand for 30 minutes. Put the mixture in a floured and greased 900 g/2 lb loaf tin and bake at 180°C/350°F/gas 4. It should be ready in an hour.

Sometimes called Irish or Scottish oatmeal, these steel-cut oats have a nutty texture.

ROUGH BROWN BREAD

The oatmeal gives this loaf a special taste and the oil makes it keep well. Pinhead oatmeal can be added to give a nutty texture.

- 350 g/12 oz/3 cups wholemeal (whole-wheat) flour
- 125 g/4 oz/1 cup white (all-purpose) flour
- 4 tbsp/5 US tbsp oatmeal
- 1 tsp/1¼ US tsp salt
- 2 tsp/2½ US tsp baking powder
- 280 ml/½ pint/1¼ cups buttermilk
- 1 large egg
- 2 tbsp/2½ US tbsp olive oil

Sift dry ingredients in the fingers. Mix the buttermilk, egg and oil together and stir into the flour mixture. Mix well and knead it a little. Cut a cross in the top. Put the dough on a baking tray at 200°C/400°F/gas 6 for 10 minutes. Reduce the heat to 190°C/375°F/gas 5 for 30 minutes, until it sounds hollow at the base. Place on a wire rack and wrap it in a clean towel to keep soft.

SALLY LUNN TEACAKE

A simple form of Sally Lunn, the classic version of which is made with yeast (page 26). These cakes are named after a girl who sold them in the streets of Bath, England, in the late eighteenth century. The recipe quickly made its way to Ireland as well as North America.

■ 125 g/4 oz/1 stick butter or margarine
■ 175 g/6 oz/¾ cup caster (superfine) sugar
■ 400 g/14 oz/3½ cups self-raising flour
■ 2 eggs, beaten
■ milk, if necessary

Cream the butter and sugar. Add the flour and beaten eggs alternately. Add a little milk if the mixture seems too stiff. Put the mixture into a well-greased tin. Bake at 220°C/425°F/gas 7 for 1 hour. Cut while still warm and spread with softened butter.

GRIDDLE BREAD

Wonderful for people in a hurry, for unexpected guests or a hungry family. It can be made with a proportion of whole-meal (whole-wheat) flour, but this will make it heavier.

■ 150 g/5 oz/1¼ cups white (all-purpose) flour
■ ½ tsp/generous ½ US tsp salt
■ ½ tsp/generous ½ US tsp bread (baking) soda
■ 150 ml/¼ pint/⅔ cup buttermilk

Mix the flour, salt and bread/baking soda in a bowl. Add the buttermilk, mixing as you pour, until the sides of the bowl are clean. Knead the dough until it is flexible. Form into a round cake, almost 2½ cm/1" high.

Sprinkle a griddle or heavy frying pan with flour and heat until the flour is pale brown. Put in the flattened dough and cook for 10 minutes on each side over a moderate heat.

Split the cake in half, spread it with soft butter and serve at once.

Yeast Breads, Buns and Rolls

White Yeast Bread (with fast-action dried yeast)
Dark Brown Bread
Wholemeal Yeast Bread
Penny Buns
Hot Cross Buns
Potato Yeast Rolls
Barm Brack
Classic Sally Lunn

Yeast is interesting stuff with strong needs of its own — these are warmth and moisture. Too much heat before the actual baking, however, will ruin everything, so success only comes with practice.

Both fresh and dried yeast need activating by mixing them with a little sugar and some warm water. After ten minutes or so, the mixture will have frothed up. It can then be stirred into some strong flour in a warmed bowl before adding more liquid, kneading and proving (leaving to rise in a warm place) for a first, and then for a second time.

In the old days, yeast was often kneaded in a losset, a wooden trough, in which it was left to prove. When I learned this, I tried kneading the dough in its own warmed bowl, then leaving it to rise in its own warmed tins. The results were excellent. We are always told to use a floured board for kneading. While adequate, this may be too draughty and inhospitable for warmth-loving yeast dough.

Life has become easier for bakers, or hopeful bakers, of yeast bread since fast-action activated yeast was invented. This is already half-way through its development and should only need one kneading and one proving, though many cooks still give it the long treatment.

Some of the recipes that follow show the long way of baking yeast bread and others the shorter one. Either way can be used. Strong flour is the best for yeast bread, and fresh yeast should only be bought if you plan to use it immediately.

Rolls made with yeast are baked on a flat baking sheet. But yeast breads, unlike country breads, are baked in loaf tins. These are the only extra pieces of equipment you will need.

WHITE YEAST BREAD
(USING FAST-ACTION DRIED YEAST)

This recipe, derived from a packet of fast-action dried yeast, produces solid but not heavy bread. It can also be made using fresh yeast or normal dried yeast, but must then be proved/raised and kneaded twice.

- 675 g/1½ lb/6 cups strong white (bread) flour
- 2 tsp/generous 2 US tsp salt
- 25 g/1 oz/2 US tsp (¼ stick) margarine or lard
- 1 x 14 g sachet fast-action dried yeast
- 450 ml/¾ pint/2 cups warm water
- (1 part boiling to 2 parts cold)

Put the flour and salt into a warm bowl. Rub in the margarine or lard. Stir in a sachet of fast-action dried yeast. Add the warm water rather slowly and mix into a dough. Turn onto a floured board and knead for 10 minutes, until very flexible. Put into 2 x 450 g/1 lb tins. Cover with oiled polythene/cling film or a clean tea towel/dish cloth and leave in a warm place to prove/raise. The dough should double its size. Bake at 200°C/400°F/gas 6 until the loaves are golden brown and sound hollow when you tap the base. Cover with a clean towel.

DARK BROWN BREAD

Dark, moist and an excellent keeper.

- 675 g/1½ lb/6 cups strong wholemeal (whole-wheat) flour
- ½ tbsp/generous ½ US tbsp salt
- 1½ tbsp/1¾ US tbsp olive oil
- ½ tbsp/generous ½ US tbsp malt extract
- 450 ml/¾ pint/2 cups warm water
- 15 g/½ oz/1 US tbsp fresh yeast *or* 7½ g/ ¼ oz/½ US tbsp dried yeast

Mix the flour and salt in a warm bowl, reserving 25 g/1 oz/2 US tbsp for kneading. Mix in the oil using a wooden spoon. Dissolve the malt extract in warm water. Crumble the yeast into the malt mixture and wait for it to become frothy, about 10 minutes. Pour the malt-yeast into the flour mixture and mix again. (You may need a little more warm water to form a dough.) When the dough is formed, knead it vigorously on a floured board for 10–15 minutes, pushing the dough with your wrists and folding it over.

Put the dough back into a warm bowl. Cover it with a clean cloth or with oiled polythene/cling film. Place the bowl somewhere warm to double the size of the dough. This may take from 40 minutes to 1 hour. Knead the dough again lightly and divide it in half. Put into 2 x 450 g/1 lb loaf tins. Place these in the warmth and cover. When the dough is about 1 cm/½" from the top of the tins, put them in the oven at 200°C/400°F/gas 6. Test after 35–40 minutes. The bread will sound hollow at the base if it is properly cooked. Put the loaves on a wire rack to cool and cover them with a cloth to keep them soft.

WHOLEMEAL YEAST BREAD

A popular bread with everyone, nourishing yet not dark or heavy.

- 675 g/1½ lb/6 cups wholemeal (whole-wheat) flour
- 450 g/1 lb/4 cups strong white (bread) flour
- 225 g/8 oz/2 cups plain (all-purpose) flour
- 1 tbsp/generous 1 US tbsp salt
- 25 g/1 oz/2 US tsp fresh yeast
- 1 tsp/1¼ US tsp sugar
- 1 L/1¾ pints/4¼ cups tepid milk and water (or plain water)

Put all the flours into a warm bowl, along with the salt. Mix the yeast and sugar until frothy, then mix with the flour. Add the tepid milk and water. Mix very well, first with a wooden spoon and then with floured hands. Knead the dough on a floured board for at least 10 minutes until it is flexible, elastic

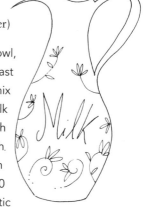

and does not stick to your hands. Put the dough into a warm bowl inside a plastic bag, or cover with a clean cloth for about 1 hour. The dough should double its size. Knead a little again and put into 2 greased loaf tins (450 g/1 lb). Put these in a warm place to rise again until the dough is near the top of the tins, about 30 minutes. Bake at 220°C/425°F/gas 7 for 10 minutes. Reduce heat to 190°C/375°F/gas 5 and bake for a further 30 minutes. The loaves are cooked when they sound hollow at the base. Cool them on a wire rack, covered with a clean cloth.

PENNY BUNS

These old-fashioned buns are much loved by children.

- 450 g/1 lb/4 cups strong white (bread) flour
- 50 g/2 oz/½ stick margarine
- 75 g/3 oz/3 US tbsp granulated sugar
- pinch of salt
- 2 tsp/2½ US tsp cinnamon
- 1 egg, beaten
- 25 g/1 oz/2 US tbsp fresh yeast
- 280 ml/½ pint/1¼ cups tepid milk and water (half and half)
- 125 g/4 oz/½ cup dried fruit
- to glaze: 1 tbsp/1¼ US tbsp each of sugar and water

In a warm bowl, rub the margarine into the flour. Add 50 g/2 oz/2 US tbsp of the sugar, and the salt and cinnamon. Mix in the beaten egg. Mix the yeast with the remaining sugar.

Add the tepid milk and water carefully. The yeast should froth. Add all of this to the flour mixture, mixing with a knife. Knead until the dough is soft, about 10 minutes. Put the dough back in the warmed bowl to rise, covered with either a plastic bag or a clean towel. It should rise in about ½ hour.

Knead the dough again and add the dried fruit, kneading all the time. Form into buns. Put on a warmed baking sheet to rise again. When the buns have risen, brush the tops with a little milk. Bake at 220°C/425°F/gas 7 for about 20 minutes. Make the glaze of water and sugar heated together. Brush this on the buns and return to the oven to harden for a minute or two.

HOT CROSS BUNS

Children love these buns traditionally made for them on Good Friday.

- 450 g/1 lb/4 cups strong white (bread) flour
- 1 tsp/1¼ US tsp salt
- 1 tsp/1¼ US tsp mixed spice
- 50 g/2 oz/½ stick butter
- 50 g/2 oz/⅓ cup currants or sultanas*
- 25 g/1 oz/2 US tbsp fresh yeast
- 50 g/2 oz/2 US tbsp sugar
- 280 ml/½ pint/1¼ cups milk

Mix the flour, salt and mixed spice in a warmed bowl. Rub in the butter and add the dried fruit. Warm the yeast, sugar and milk. Keep at blood heat for 10 minutes, then mix with flour mixture to form a dough. Knead for 10 minutes or until dough is flexible. Put it back in bowl. Cover with a clean, damp cloth until it doubles its size — about 1 hour. Put onto a floured board and knead lightly. Divide into bun shapes, tucking sides under to avoid spreading. Flatten, then mark deeply on the top with a cross. Leave in a warm place for 20 minutes. Bake at 200°C/400°F/gas 6 for 20 minutes. Brush over with a sugar-water glaze while still warm.

Sultanas are dried green grapes and are usually larger and juicier than raisins.

POTATO YEAST ROLLS

Theodora FitzGibbon, Ireland's classic cookery writer, was enthusiastic about these rolls. They are well worth the careful preparation they need and will also freeze well.

- 125 g/4 oz/¾ cup potatoes
- 1 tsp/1¼ US tsp salt
- 25 g/1 oz/2 US tbsp fresh yeast *or*
- 15 g/½ oz/1 US tbsp dried yeast
- 50 g/2 oz/ 2 US tbsp sugar
- 450 g/1 lb/4 cups warm white (all-purpose) flour
- 50 g/2 oz/½ stick butter
- 140 ml/¼ pint/⅔ cup warm milk
- 140 ml/¼ pint/⅔ cup water
- 1 egg, beaten
- milk for glazing

Cook the potatoes in salted water and drain, reserving 2 tbsp/2½ US tbsp of the cooking liquid. Mash the potatoes very well. Cover and keep warm. Cream the yeast in a bowl with the reserved tepid potato liquid and half the sugar. It must be frothing up when mixed well. Sift the flour into a large warmed mixing bowl and rub in the butter. Make a well in the centre and add the rest of the sugar and the mashed potatoes. Mix well. Add the warm milk and the water to the yeast liquid. Mix and add to the mixing bowl, then beat in the beaten egg. Knead for at least 10 minutes.

Leave in a warm place, covered with a clean tea towel/dish cloth for 1 hour, by which time it should have doubled its size. Turn onto a flat surface and shape into rolls. Put these on a greased baking sheet. They will rise after 20 minutes in a warm place, covered with a clean tea towel/dish cloth. Brush with milk and bake at 200°C/400°F/gas 6 for 15–20 minutes. Arrange on a wire rack to cool.

BARM BRACK

In Irish, *bairin breac* means speckled yeast bread. It is the traditional bread for Hallowe'en.

- 450 g/1 lb/4 cups strong white (bread) flour
- a pinch of salt
- 15 g/½ oz/1 US tbsp dried yeast dissolved in
- 3 tbsp/3¾ US tbsp warm water
- 280 ml/½ pint/1¼ cups milk
- 50 g/2 oz/½ stick butter
- 50 g/2 oz/¼ cup sugar
- 1 egg, beaten
- 225 g/8 oz/1¼ cups sultanas*
- 125 g/4 oz/generous ½ cup candied peel
- a little cinnamon and coriander (optional)
- sugar and water for glaze

Put flour and salt into bowl. Sprinkle the dried yeast on the warm water. Warm the milk and butter until tepid. Add the yeast mixture, sugar and egg to the flour. Then add the warmed milk mixture and mix well.

Empty the mixture onto a floured board and knead for 15 minutes. Put into a warm bowl and cover until double its size. This may take an hour or longer. Empty the dough back onto a floured board. Knead well again, adding the fruit and mixing until all the fruit is absorbed.

Put the dough into a greased and lined 22 cm/9" cake tin. Place the tin in a warm place and cover with a clean, damp cloth. The dough should rise in about 20 minutes. Place in the centre of oven at 200°C/400°F/gas 6 for 50 minutes. If the base is still pale after this time, turn the brack over and bake for another 5 minutes.

Make a sugar and water glaze, brush over and put back in the oven for a few minutes to harden. Put on a wire rack and cover with a clean cloth until cool.

A little cinnamon and coriander also taste good in a barm brack.

Sultanas are dried green grapes and are usually larger and juicier than raisins.

CLASSIC SALLY LUNN

Legend says that Sally Lunn sold her wonderful teacake in the streets of Bath, England, in the late 1700s. Now her teacake is known in Britain and America as well as Ireland. I have a recipe for a Sally Lunn yeast cake from a manuscript dated 1829 and found in the rafters of an old house in County Dublin.

Sally Lunn teacake was always a treat. It was sliced horizontally and spread thickly with butter. Then the halves were put together again and the teacake was sliced downwards. The butter melted deliciously. To keep it hot, it was placed by an open fire on a trivet, usually a brass one.

This recipe is made from fast-action yeast. If you choose to use fresh yeast, check the instructions on the packet.

- 350 g/12 oz/3 cups strong white (bread) flour
- 50 g/2 oz/½ stick margarine
- ½ tsp/generous ½ US tsp sugar
- 15 g/½ oz/1 US tbsp fast-action yeast
- 1 egg, beaten
- 175 ml/6 oz/¾ cup tepid milk

Rub the margarine into the flour. Add the sugar and yeast. Then add the beaten egg and the tepid milk. Mix well and then knead on a floured board for 10 minutes. Halve the kneaded mixture and put it into two round 20 cm/7" tins. Prove/raise in a warm place, covering the tins with oiled polythene bags. When the dough has risen, in about 20 minutes, bake for 20 minutes at 220°C/425°F/gas 7. Brush with milk to glaze and return to the oven to dry for 5 minutes.

Fruit Breads

Banana Fruit Loaf
Cherry Loaf
Date and Walnut Loaf
Nutty Fruit Slices
Fruit and Orange Bread
Brack
Malt Bread
Spiced Sultana Bread

Fruit bread or 'brack' was always a popular bread for special occasions. The most famous of these is Barm Brack, meaning fruit bread made with yeast (page 24). Barm is Irish for 'yeast'. Brack means 'speckled'.

Most people did not and still do not make the yeast brack. They make excellent fruit breads by pouring boiling water over the sultanas and candied peel, or by soaking the dried fruit in cold tea overnight before starting to make the mixture. In the old days, this was baked in a pot oven.

The recipes include the old-fashioned fruit breads, or 'bracks' that have always been popular, as well as some modern versions. Dates, bananas and oranges are now commonly used in fruit breads, giving them a light, natural moisture; the nuts give them crunchiness.

A different taste entirely is malt. Malt extract gives flour a rich flavour and mixes well with any kind of fruit, especially that delicious ingredient, candied peel.

People who like fruit bread but who are in a hurry should try the fruit slices on page 31. They are crisp and whole-some and ready to eat soon after baking. For these you will need a Swiss roll tin or high-sided cookie sheet. Otherwise, fruit breads are best made in loaf tins.

BANANA FRUIT LOAF

A simple fruit loaf which can be made quickly. The banana makes it unusually refreshing.

- 175 g/6 oz/1½ cups white self-raising flour
- 75 g/3 oz/½ cup soft brown sugar
- 125 g/4 oz/1 cup dried fruit (mixed sultanas and candied peel)
- 1 egg, beaten
- 2 bananas, mashed well

Mix the flour, sugar and dried fruit in a bowl. Add the beaten egg and mix. Add the well-mashed bananas. Mix thoroughly until very soft. Press the mixture into a greased and half-lined 450 g/1 lb loaf tin. Bake at 190°C/375°F/gas 5 for 45 minutes. Cool the loaf in the tin and then put it on a wire rack.

CHERRY LOAF

The Irish have a weakness for glacé cherries. This loaf tastes best when sliced and spread thinly with softened butter. Candied peel can be substituted for a proportion of the cherries.

- 125 g/4 oz/1 cup white self-raising flour
- pinch of salt
- 125 g/4 oz/1 cup ground almonds
- 125 g/4 oz/1 stick butter or margarine
- 125 g/4 oz/½ cup sugar
- 2 eggs, beaten
- 225 g/8 oz/2 cups glacé cherries, halved

Mix the flour, salt and ground almonds and set aside. Cream the butter and sugar, then mix in the beaten egg. Add the flour mixture and mix well. Then add the cherries.

When well mixed, turn into a greased 900 g/2 lb loaf tin. Bake for 1 hour at 190°C/375°F/gas 5 for approximately 55 minutes. Cool in the tin for at least 10 minutes before turning onto a wire rack.

DATE AND WALNUT LOAF

A date loaf that is quickly prepared, helped by the melting method. Like everything made with dates, it will remain moist for some days.

- 225 g/8 oz/1¼ cups dates, chopped
- 200 ml/7 oz/⅔ cup boiling water
- 125 g/4 oz/1 stick margarine
- 50 g/2 oz/½ cup walnuts, well chopped
- 200 g/7 oz/⅔ cup sugar
- 275 g/10 oz/2½ cups white (all-purpose) flour
- 1 egg, beaten
- 1 tsp/1¼ US tsp bread (baking) soda
- a little milk

Soak the chopped dates in the boiling water in a large saucepan for 15 minutes. Add the margarine and let it melt. When this has cooled (about 10 minutes), add the chopped walnuts, sugar, flour and beaten egg. Mix the bread/baking soda with a little milk. Add to the mixture and stir well.

Line the base of 2 x 450 g/1 lb loaf tins with tin foil and grease the sides. Bake at 180°–200°C/ 350–400°F/gas 4–6 for 1 hour and 10 minutes. Cool the loaves in the tins and then put on a wire rack.

NUTTY FRUIT SLICES

A crisp change from fruit bread. Use any combination of fruit you like.

- 175 g/6 oz/1½ sticks margarine
- 125 g/4 oz/½ cup sugar
- 2 level dsp/3 US tbsp golden (Karo) syrup
- 150 g/5 oz/1¼ cups white self-raising flour
- 150 g/5 oz/1¼ cups wholemeal (whole-wheat) self-raising flour
- 125 g/4 oz/⅔ cup sultanas*
- 50 g/2 oz/½ cup walnuts, chopped
- 50 g/2 oz/½ cup cherries, chopped
- caster (superfine) sugar to sprinkle

Melt margarine, sugar and syrup in a large saucepan. *Do not let it boil.* Add flours, sultanas, nuts and cherries and mix well. Spread the mixture into a Swiss roll tin/high-sided cookie sheet. Bake at 180°C/350°F/gas 4 for about 20 minutes.

Cut into slices while still warm and sprinkle with caster (superfine) sugar. Separate the slices when they are cold.

Sultanas are dried green grapes and are usually larger and juicier than raisins.

FRUIT AND ORANGE BREAD

The orange gives this bread an exotic flavour.

- 225 g/8 oz/1¼ cups fruit (candied peel, sultanas* or raisins, chopped dates)
- 175 ml/6 oz/⅔ cup cold tea
- 175 g/6 oz/⅔ cup brown sugar
- 50 g/2 oz/½ stick butter
- grated rind of 1 orange
- 2 tbsp/2½ US tbsp freshly-squeezed orange juice
- 1 egg, beaten
- 225 g/8 oz/2 cups white self-raising flour
- 1 rounded tsp/1¼ US tsp cinnamon

Soak fruit in the cold tea overnight. Heat the fruit mixture and add the sugar and butter, stirring until they dissolve. Add the orange rind and juice. Cool. Add the egg. Add the flour and cinnamon.

Pour the mixture into a 450 g/1 lb greased and lined loaf tin and bake at 180°C/350°F/gas 4 for 1 hour and 20 minutes.

Sultanas are dried green grapes and are usually larger and juicier than raisins.

BRACK

This is a simple version of the more complicated and traditional barm brack. A similar brack can be made by soaking
the dried fruit in cold tea overnight before mixing in the
flour.

- 225 g/8 oz/2 cups dried fruit (sultanas* and candied peel)
- 1 tsp salt
- 1 tsp/1¼ US tsp bread (baking) soda
- 225 ml/8 oz/1 cup boiling water
- 225 g/8 oz/2 cups white (all-purpose) flour
- 125 g/4 oz/½ cup dark or medium brown sugar
- 1 tsp/1¼ US tsp mixed spice or cinnamon

Mix the fruit, salt and bread/baking soda in a bowl. Pour
the boiling water over this. Leave for 10 minutes to soften
the fruit. Add the flour, sugar and spice. Mix everything to
a dropping consistency.

Put it in a greased 450 g/1 lb loaf tin. Bake at 190°C/
375°F/gas 4 for approximately ¾ hour. Cool the brack in
the tin for a while before turning onto a wire rack.

*Sultanas are dried green grapes and are usually larger and juicier
than raisins.

MALT BREAD

A bread with an unusual flavour which keeps very well.

- 225 g/8 oz/2 cups white (all-purpose) flour
- ½ tsp bread (baking) soda
- 2 tsp/2½ US tsp baking powder
- ½ tsp salt
- 75 g/3 oz/¾ cup sultanas*
- 50 g/2 oz/½ cup candied peel
- 25 g/1 oz/¼ stick margarine
- 2 tbsp/2½ US tbsp malt extract
- 2 tbsp/2½US tbsp brown sugar
- 280 ml/½ pint/1¼ cups milk

Mix the flour, bread/baking soda, baking powder, salt, sultanas and candied peel in a bowl. Heat the margarine, malt extract, brown sugar and milk. Cool a little. Mix with the dry ingredients to a dropping consistency.

Bake in a greased and lined 450 g/1 lb loaf tin at 200°C/400°F/gas 6. Test after 30 minutes. Cool in the tin, then place it on a wire rack. Wrap in a clean cloth.

*Sultanas are dried green grapes and are usually larger and juicier than raisins.

SPICED SULTANA BREAD

This popular fruit bread is an excellent keeper. Any combination of fruits or spices can be used.

- 275 g/10 oz/2½ cups white self-raising flour
- 1 tsp/1¼ US tsp mixed spice
- ½ tsp ground ginger
- 125 g/4 oz/½ cup demerara (granulated brown) sugar
- 50 g/2 oz/½ cup candied peel
- 175 g/6 oz/1½ cups sultanas*
- 125 g/4 oz/1 stick butter or margarine
- 175 ml/6 oz/¾ cup golden (Karo) syrup
- 1 large egg, beaten
- 4 tbsp/5 US tbsp milk

Sift the flour, mixed spice and ginger in your fingers. Add the demerara (granulated brown) sugar and fruits. Melt the syrup and butter together. Make a well in the dry ingredients and mix in the butter–syrup. Add the beaten egg and milk and mix well.

Pour the mixture into a greased and lined 900 g/2 lb loaf tin and bake at 160°C/325°F/gas 3. Do not open the oven door for 40 minutes. This loaf will take about 1¼ hours to cook through. Cool it in the tin for 15 minutes before putting it on a wire rack.

Sultanas are dried green grapes and are usually larger and juicier than raisins.

Scones and Potato Cakes

Brown Scones
White Scones
Drop Scones
Nutty Brown Scones
Oat Cakes
Boxty Pancakes
Potato Cakes

When unexpected guests came, the cook had to work quickly. No one was allowed to leave even the most modest house without being given a cup of tea and some freshly-baked morsels to eat. This is where scones came into their own.

If the oven was already hot (the range was always going, winter or summer), a mixture could be put together in five minutes and baked in ten more. The scones in these recipes were popular for this and were split and filled with melting butter.

If there was no hot oven, a griddle would be greased and heated over the open fire. When the griddle was hot, in would go spoonfuls of a pancake mixture for drop scones, or flat potato patties for potato cakes. Boxty pancakes, a strange mixture of cooked and raw potato, flour and egg, required a special skill. They were baked on the griddle on All Saints' Day.

A heavy frying pan is a good substitute for a griddle. As with the oven-baked scones, the griddle cakes should be eaten immediately with fresh butter.

BROWN SCONES

These crisp, nutty little scones are delicious served warm with country butter.

- 125 g/4 oz/1 cup wholemeal (whole-wheat) flour
- 125 g/4 oz/1 cup plain (all-purpose) flour
- ¾ tsp/generous ¾ US tsp bread (baking) soda
- 1 dsp/1½ US tbsp sugar
- pinch of salt
- 115 ml/4 oz/½ cup buttermilk

Mix all the dry ingredients in a bowl. Add the buttermilk. Knead slightly until the dough is elastic. Roll the dough out to 1 cm/½" thick on a floured board. Cut into rounds about 5 cm/2" in diameter. Bake at 230°C/425°F/gas 7 for 15 minutes.

WHITE SCONES

My friend Nora has baked these melting scones for many years. They are light and should be small in diameter, just big enough for one or two mouthfuls. They are delicious eaten on the day they are baked, served with butter and homemade jam.

- 225 g/8 oz/2 cups self-raising white flour
- pinch of salt
- 50 g/2 oz/½ stick margarine
- 2 tbsp/2½ US tbsp white sugar
- 1 egg, beaten
- 3 tbsp/3¾ US tbsp milk

Mix the flour and salt in a large bowl. Cut the margarine in small pieces and rub into the flour. Add the sugar. Add the beaten egg gradually, then the milk. The mixture should become a soft dough. Knead it quickly on a floured board. Roll out to 1½ cm/½" thick. Cut out 5 cm/2" rounds. Place the scones on a greased baking sheet and bake at 220°C/425°F/gas 7 for 12–15 minutes. Cool on the baking sheet and then put them on a wire rack.

DROP SCONES

These well-known favourites have several names. Some people call them buttermilk pancakes, others crumpets. In Scotland, they are called girdle cakes. Delicious for tea in winter, they can be cooked in a heavy frying pan. Drop scones can also be made with fresh milk.

- 225 g/8 oz/2 cups white (all-purpose) flour
- ½ tsp/generous ½ US tsp bread (baking) soda
- ½ tsp/generous ½ US tsp Bextartar or cream of tartar
- 2 eggs, beaten
- 280 ml/½ pint/1¼ cups buttermilk

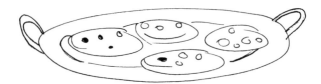

Mix the flour, bread/baking soda and cream of tartar in a bowl. Stir in the beaten eggs, then the buttermilk. Mix everything well. Grease a griddle or heavy frying pan. Heat it very well, then reduce the heat a little. Drop spoonfuls of the scone mixture onto the hot griddle. When bubbles appear on the surface, turn them over.

When the scones are golden brown on both sides, they are cooked. At this stage, put them into a clean tea towel/dish cloth to keep them warm and steamy. Serve hot with softened butter or with a sprinkling of sugar and lemon juice.

NUTTY BROWN SCONES

These scones should be shaped with a small cutter.

- 275 g/10 oz/2½ cups white (all-purpose) flour
- 150 g/5 oz/1¼ cups wholemeal (whole-wheat) flour
- 1 tbsp/1¼ US tbsp pinhead oatmeal*
- 1 tsp bread (baking) soda
- ½ tsp salt
- 1 tsp cream of tartar
- 50 g/2 oz/½ stick butter
- 225 g/8 oz/1 cup buttermilk

Mix all the dry ingredients. Rub in the butter. Add the buttermilk and knead the dough well. Roll out to 1 cm/½" thick. Brush with milk. Cut into rounds and bake at 220°C/425°F/gas 7 for 15–20 minutes.

*Sometimes called Irish or Scottish oatmeal, these steel-cut oats have a nutty texture.

OAT CAKES

Hearty, sustaining and crunchy. Oat cakes baked in the oven taste better than those done on a greased griddle.

- 125 g/4 oz/1 cup oatmeal
- 125 g/4 oz/1 cup white (all-purpose) flour
- 1 tsp salt
- 1 tsp/1¼ US tsp baking powder
- 125 g/4 oz/1 stick butter or margarine
- 50 ml/2 oz/¼ cup hot water

Mix the oatmeal, flour, salt and baking powder. Melt the butter in the hot water and add it to the dry ingredients. Knead the dough a little on a floured board. Roll thinly. Cut into 'farls' or quarters or stamp into rounds with a cutter. Either cook on both sides on a greased griddle, or bake in oven at 180°C/350°F/gas 4 for 25 minutes. Eat the same day with farm butter and honey.

BOXTY PANCAKES

These are traditional potato pancakes. In the past, with shops so far away, they were well known as welcoming food for unexpected visitors. They were more popular in northern counties. A griddle or a heavy frying pan should be used to produce the authentic flavour and texture.

- 450 g/1 lb potatoes, peeled
- 175 g/6 oz/1½ cups white (all-purpose) flour
- ½ tsp baking powder
- pinch of salt

- 1 egg, beaten
- 125 ml/4 oz/½ cup milk (more may be needed to make a dropping consistency)
- a little butter for the frying pan

Sieve/sift the flour, baking powder and salt into a large bowl. Boil and mash half of the potatoes. Grate remaining potatoes. Wring the grated potato in a clean towel to squeeze out excess water. Add all potatoes to the dry ingredients. Mix in the beaten egg and milk gradually, adding more milk if necessary. The mixture should be the consistency of batter.

Drop dessertspoons/tablespoons of this onto the hot, greased griddle. Cook the pancakes for about 5 minutes on each side or until they are brown. Serve immediately with butter and salt. They taste good with fried rashers/slices of bacon too.

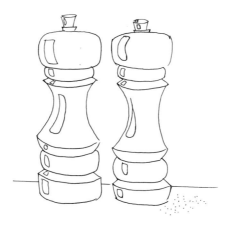

POTATO CAKES

An age-old and much-loved Irish food. Potato cakes can be eaten hot with a knob of butter melting over them for tea. They are also delicious with fried bacon and eggs for breakfast or lunch. Children love them!

- 175 g/6 oz/1 cup mashed potato
- 125 g/4 oz/1 cup self-raising white flour
- 50 g/2 oz/½ stick butter
- extra butter for cooking

Steam or boil the potatoes. Mash them without using milk. Rub the butter into the flour. Mix this well with the mashed potato and knead it into a flexible dough. Either roll the dough on a pastry board and cut it into rounds, or less wastefully, form it into several flat cakes with your hands.

Melt a little butter in a hot frying pan or a griddle and put in the potato cakes. Cook them on both sides until they are dry and golden brown. Serve at once with softened butter.

Biscuits/Cookies

Shortbread Fingers
Portarlington Golden Biscuits
Porter Hope Biscuits
Apple Fingers
Hunting Nuts
Orange and Lemon Biscuits
Oatmeal Biscuits
Ginger Biscuits

Homemade biscuits were always good to taste but could be tedious to make. There was the mixing, kneading, rolling on a floured board, stamping out the biscuits and dealing with the always difficult remains and a lot of cleaning up.

Of the eight recipes on our list, only two need rolling and cutting, or stamping out — the orange and lemon biscuits (our only party ones), and the hunting nuts (amusing leftovers from long ago).

Otherwise these biscuits are mixed by the now-popular 'melting method'. Depending on the recipes, margarine or butter is softened at the side of a stove and everything meltable is mixed with it. When all is liquid, it is poured onto the flour mixture to make a dough. This dough is either pressed into that invaluable thing, a Swiss roll tin, or else dropped on baking sheets in small rounds.

The melting method takes only a quarter of the time and energy of the old-fashioned way and no extra equipment is needed.

SHORTBREAD FINGERS

Shortbread used to be made slowly, even painfully, by rubbing and kneading. This new melting method is far quicker and easier, and the shortbread could not be better. Delicious, melting and crumbly.

- 125 g/4 oz/1 stick butter
- 125 g/4 oz/1 stick margarine
- 250 g/9 oz/2¼ cups white (all-purpose) flour
- 75 g/3 oz/¾ cup cornflour (corn starch)
- 75 g/3 oz/3 US tbsp caster (superfine) sugar

Melt the butter and margarine very slowly in a large saucepan. Sieve/sift the dry ingredients and add them to the melted butter and margarine. Mix to a dough using a wooden spoon. Press the dough into a greased Swiss roll tin/high-sided cookie sheet. Smooth it with a knife and prick it all over with a carving fork. Bake at 190°C/375°F/gas 5 for about 25 minutes or until pale brown.

Mark the shortbread into fingers while it is warm and dredge with caster (superfine) sugar. Turn onto a wire rack when it is nearly cold.

PORTARLINGTON GOLDEN BISCUITS

These golden biscuits are both popular and simple to make.

- 175 g/6 oz/1½ cups self-raising white flour
- ½ tsp bread (baking) soda
- 125 g/4 oz/1 stick margarine
- 1 dsp/1½ US tbsp golden (Karo) syrup
- 75 g/3 oz/3 US tbsp sugar

Mix the flour and bread/baking soda in a bowl. Melt the margarine and golden/Karo syrup in a saucepan. Add the sugar. When the sugar is dissolved, bring the melted ingredients to the boil. Pour the melted mixture onto the flour. Stir well with a wooden spoon.

Flour your hands and make balls measuring 2½ cm/1" in diameter out of the dough. Put these on a greased baking sheet and bake at 200°C/400°F/gas 6 for 10–15 minutes or until golden brown. Cool on a wire rack.

PORTER HOPE BISCUITS

This recipe makes a surprising number — about 3 dozen — of these delicious biscuits.

- 350 g/12 oz/3¼ cups white (all-purpose) flour
- 1 tsp/generous 1 US tsp cream of tartar
- ½ tsp/generous ½ US tsp bread (baking) soda
- 225 g/8 oz/2 sticks butter
- 225 g/8 oz/1 cup caster (superfine) sugar
- 1 egg, beaten

Mix the flour, cream of tartar and bread/baking soda in a bowl. Rub in the butter and then the sugar. Put in the egg and, using your hands, mix everything into a solid mass.

Break up the dough into walnut-sized pieces and flatten these out into small biscuit shapes. They will spread out during baking. Arrange the pieces on a greased baking tray and bake at 180°C/350°F/gas 4 for approximately 20 minutes. Cool for a few minutes, then put them onto a wire rack.

APPLE FINGERS

Half biscuits and half cakes, these apple fingers can also be reheated and served with cream as a simple pudding. 50 g/ 2 oz/2 cup of candied peel or chopped walnuts could also be added to this mixture.

- 275 g/10 oz/2½ cups self-raising white flour
- 150 g/5 oz/1¼ sticks margarine or butter
- 150 g/5 oz/⅔ cup brown sugar
- 1 tsp/1½ US tsp cinnamon
- 1 cooking apple, finely chopped or grated
- 1 egg, beaten
- 1 tbsp/1½ US tbsp milk
- caster (superfine) sugar to sprinkle over

Rub the margarine or butter into the flour. Add the brown sugar and the cinnamon. Add the apple and mix very well. Add the beaten egg and milk to make a softish dough. Spread the mixture into a well-greased Swiss roll tin/high-sided cookie sheet. Bake at 200°C/400°F/gas 6 for 30 minutes, turning the tin once, until golden brown. Place the tin on a wire rack and sprinkle the mixture with caster (superfine) sugar. Mark it into fingers while it is hot and cut them when it is cool. Put the fingers on a wire rack before storing in a tin.

HUNTING NUTS

Many years ago, these fortifying biscuits were made for huntsmen. Their long flat shape, like a bar of chocolate, makes them fit easily into a coat pocket. Long and solid, they are wonderful for the outdoor life as they do not crumble and will survive any amount of jolting.

- 200 g/7 oz/1¼ cups white (all-purpose) flour
- 25 g/1 oz/½ cup oatmeal
- 50 g/2 oz/½ cup candied peel
- pinch of ginger
- pinch of mixed spice
- pinch of bread (baking) soda
- 175 ml/6 oz/¾ cup black treacle (molasses)
- 75 g/3 oz/⅔ stick butter and margarine, mixed
- 50 g/2 oz/¼ cup caster (superfine) sugar

Mix the flour, oatmeal, candied peel, spices and bread/baking soda in a bowl. Melt the treacle/molasses, butter and caster (superfine) sugar in a saucepan. Mix this with the dry ingredients and knead it lightly into a hard ball. Put aside for 4 hours.

Roll the dough out carefully on a floured board. When it is ½ cm/¼" thick, cut it into rectangles of about 7 cm x 3 cm/ 3" x 1½". Bake at 200°C/400°F/gas 6 for 8–10 minutes. Cool on the baking sheet before putting onto a wire rack.

ORANGE AND LEMON BISCUITS

Very pretty for a special occasion, these biscuits are for
people who like sweet things.

- 140 g/4½ oz/1 stick + 1 US tbsp margarine
- 140 g/4½ oz/½ cup sugar
- 250 g/9 oz/2¼ cups white (all-purpose) flour
- grated rind of 1 orange
- grated rind of ½ lemon
- 2 eggs, beaten
- orange juice, icing (confectioners') sugar, candied peel

Beat the margarine and sugar to a cream. Add the flour
and the orange and lemon rind. Mix well and add the light-
ly-beaten eggs. Knead lightly until the dough is soft and
elastic.

Roll out the dough to ½ cm/¼" thick on a floured board.
Cut into small rounds. Bake at 200°C/400°F/gas 6 for
15–20 minutes. Allow the biscuits to harden, then put them
on a wire rack.

Make a thick syrup with the orange juice and icing/confec-
tioners' sugar and spread it on the biscuits when they are
cold. Scatter a little candied peel over the icing while it is
still soft.

OATMEAL BISCUITS

Crunchy and wholesome, this recipe makes 2 dozen biscuits.

- 125 g/4 oz/1 cup white (all-purpose) flour
- 125 g/4 oz/1 cup oatmeal
- 125 g/4 oz/1 stick margarine
- 75 g/3 oz/⅓ cup demerara (granulated brown) sugar
- 1 dsp/1½ US tbsp golden (Karo) syrup
- small tsp water
- ½ tsp bread (baking) soda

Put the flour and oatmeal into a bowl. Put the margarine, sugar, syrup and water into a saucepan and warm it until it is melted. Add the bread/baking soda. Pour this mixture into the dry ingredients and stir very well with a wooden spoon. Shape into small morsels on baking trays and bake for 15 minutes at 180°C/350°F/gas 4. Cool on the baking tray and put them on a wire rack when cool.

GINGER BISCUITS

Golden brown and slightly brittle.

- 175 g/6 oz/1½ cups white (all-purpose) flour
- 125 g/4 oz/½ cup sugar
- ½ tsp/generous ½ US tsp baking powder
- ½ tsp/generous ½ US tsp bread (baking) soda
- 2 tsp/2½ US tsp ground ginger
- 50 g/2 oz/½ stick margarine or butter
- 40 ml/1½ oz/1½ US tbsp golden (Karo) syrup
- 1 egg, beaten
- 1 tbsp/1½ US tbsp milk

Mix all the dry ingredients well in a bowl. Melt the margarine or butter and syrup in a saucepan. Add this to the dry ingredients, mixing well. Add the beaten egg and milk.

Sprinkle flour over the well-mixed dough and flour your hands. Knead well until the dough is soft and pliable. Arrange the mixture on a baking tray in walnut-size pieces. These will spread in the oven.

Bake at 180°C/350°F/gas 4 for 15–20 minutes. Cool the biscuits on the tray for a few minutes before putting them on a wire rack.

Cakes

Madeira Cake
Irish Marmalade Cake
Irish Apple Cake
Apple Cinnamon Cake
Lemon Cake
Irish Whiskey Cake
Irish Porter Cake
Aunt Mollie's Simple Fruitcake
Christmas Cake

Cakes were always produced on special occasions in Ireland and many of them were baked in pot ovens. Even a Madeira cake could be cooked very well in a pot oven.

Apples were used a great deal in cake-making in the autumn and winter months. Dried fruit was substituted when the fresh had been used up. Christmas cake was cooked very slowly and packed tightly with dried fruit. It was eaten on Christmas Eve and made of the same mixture as traditional Irish wedding and christening cakes. The recipes were handed down from mother to daughter.

There was not time in the homes to make rich, creamy cakes like those we see in shops. To enrich the cake mixtures, people used whiskey, stout or lemon. Porter or whiskey cake was served with tea after the Christmas goose.

Traditionally, cakes were always round, although this has changed lately. Lemon, Madeira and fruit cakes are now baked in rectangular loaf tins. The cakes bake through better in a loaf tin. And if the tin needs lining, this is also more easily done if it is rectangular.

MADEIRA CAKE

The classic Madeira cake was so called because stylish people once ate a slice while drinking a glass of Madeira at noon. In those days, about one hundred and fifty years ago, the fashion was to have a large breakfast at 10 am and dinner in the early evening at 5.30.

In country cottages, Madeira cake was sometimes made in a skillet over the open fire.

- 175 g/6 oz/1½ cups self-raising white flour
- 165 g/5½ oz/⅔ cup sugar
- 1 tsp/1¼ US tsp baking powder
- 125 g/4 oz/1 stick butter
- 3 eggs, beaten
- 2 tbsp/2½ US tbsp milk

Sift the flour and sugar in your fingers and add the baking powder. Cream the butter. Mix the dry ingredients into the creamed butter. Add the well-beaten eggs and milk. Beat well for 3 minutes. Pour the mixture into a well-greased and lined loaf tin. Bake at 200°C/400°F/gas 6 for 1 hour, or until firm to the touch and golden brown. A Madeira cake should stay moist for a week.

IRISH MARMALADE CAKE

An Irish marmalade cake has more flavour when made with a liqueur marmalade. It tastes especially good when spread thinly with softened butter.

- 125 g/4 oz/1 stick butter
- 125 g/4 oz/½ cup sugar
- 125 g/4 oz/4 US tbsp whiskey marmalade (Irish Mist, if possible)
- 225 g/8 oz/2 cups self-raising white flour
- 2 eggs, beaten
- 2 tbsp/2½ US tbsp milk

Cream the butter and sugar. Add the marmalade and beat well. Add the flour, beaten eggs and milk bit by bit. Spread the mixture in a greased 20 cm/7½" tin lined with tin foil.

Bake for about 1 hour at 190–200°C/375–400°F/ gas 5–6. Keep in the tin until it is cool.

IRISH APPLE CAKE

This sandwich cake can also serve as a pudding when smothered with cream or sprinkled with caster (superfine) sugar.

- 200 g/7 oz/1¼ cups self-raising white flour
- 125 g/4 oz/1 stick butter or margarine
- 75 g/3 oz/⅓ cup sugar
- 1 egg, beaten
- 1 tbsp/1½ US tbsp milk
- 1 large cooking apple, sliced
- 1 tsp/1¼ US tsp cinnamon

Rub the butter into the flour. Add all but 1 tbsp of the sugar. Add the beaten egg slowly. Mix well. Add the milk and mix again. Form the mixture into a dough and knead it slightly with floury fingers until it is soft and pliable. Divide it into 2 pieces.

Roll one piece on a floured board and place it in a tart plate/pie dish. Spread the apple slices over the dough. Sprinkle the cinnamon and the remaining sugar over the apple slices. Cover with the second piece of dough, rolled out to fit over the first. Press the edges down. Cut 2 or 3 vents on the top and brush with any remaining beaten egg.

Bake at 180°C/350°F/gas 4 for approximately 35 minutes, until golden brown.

APPLE CINNAMON CAKE

Spicy and moist, this cake can be eaten hot with cream, or spread with butter when cold. Chopped walnuts could be substituted for half of the candied peel.

- 200 g/7 oz/1¼ cups self-raising white flour
- 125 g/4 oz/1 stick margarine or butter
- 75 g/3 oz/⅓ cup sugar
- 1 tsp/1¼ US tsp coriander
- 1 dsp/1½ US tbsp cinnamon
- 50 g/2 oz/½ cup mixed peel
- 1 cooking apple, thinly sliced
- 1 egg, beaten
- 2 tbsp/2½ US tbsp milk

Sift the flour into a large bowl. Cut the margarine into small pieces and rub into the flour. Stir in the sugar, cinnamon, coriander and peel. Mix in the apple slices. Stir in the beaten egg and milk using a wooden spoon. Knead lightly until the dough is elastic. Place in a cake tin and bake at 200°C/400°F/gas 6 for 35 minutes. Cover with tin foil if the cake shows signs of burning and lower the temperature slightly if necessary.

LEMON CAKE

Lemon cake is genuinely refreshing. It is a strong butter-yellow colour and keeps for several days.

THE BATTER

- 125 g/4 oz/1 stick butter
- 175 g/6 oz/³⁄₄ cup caster (superfine) sugar
- grated rind of 1 lemon
- 2 eggs, beaten
- 175 g/6 oz/1½ cups self-raising white flour
- a little milk

THE SAUCE

- juice of the grated lemon
- 50 g/2 oz/¼ cup granulated sugar

Cream the butter, caster (superfine) sugar and lemon rind. Add the beaten eggs and the flour. Add a little milk until the mixture is a dropping consistency. Spread in a greased and lined loaf tin. Bake for 45–50 minutes at 190–200°C/ 375–400°F/ gas 5–6. Warm the mixture of lemon juice and granulated sugar. As soon as the cake comes out of the oven, prick the surface well and pour on the lemon-sugar mixture. Leave the cake in the tin to cool.

IRISH WHISKEY CAKE

Light but moist, this cake is especially attractive if made in a ring tin.

THE CAKE

- 175 g/6 oz/1½ sticks margarine (Flora is best for creaming)
- 175 g/6 oz/¾ cup caster (superfine) sugar
- 175 g/6 oz/1½ cups white flour
- 175 g/6 oz/1 cup sultanas (dried green grapes)
- 3 eggs, beaten
- 2 tbsp/2½ US tbsp Irish whiskey
- ½ level tsp baking powder

THE ICING

- 175 g/6 oz/1½ cups icing (confectioners') sugar
- juice of 1 orange
- a little candied peel

Cream the margarine and sugar in a large bowl. Add the sifted flour and the sultanas gradually. Add the eggs and mix well. Add the whiskey. Add the baking powder, folding it in gently. Mix carefully to a dropping consistency. Put into a greased ring tin or greased and lined loaf tin. Bake at 180°C/350°F/gas 4 for 1 hour. In a ring tin, this will bake in 30 minutes at 200°C/400°F/gas 6.

Make the icing from the icing/confectioners' sugar dissolved in the orange juice. Spread this over the cake and scatter a little candied peel over the icing.

IRISH PORTER CAKE

An excellent keeper, Irish porter cake is nut-brown and lighter in texture than most fruit cakes.

- 150 g/5 oz/1¼ sticks margarine
- 150 g/5 oz/¾ cup brown sugar
- 190 ml/⅓ pint/⅓ cup Guinness
- 450 g/1 lb/3 cups sultanas*
- 75 g/3 oz/⅔ cup candied peel
- 400 g/14 oz/3½ cups white (all-purpose) flour
- ½ tsp/generous ½ US tsp bread (baking) soda
- 1½ tsp/1¼ US tsp cinnamon
- 2 eggs, beaten

Put the margarine, sugar and Guinness into a saucepan and bring gently to the boil. Stir the mixture until all is melted and dissolved. Add the fruit and the candied peel and let everything simmer for 5 minutes. Cool to blood heat.

Meanwhile, sieve/sift the flour, bread/baking soda and cinnamon into a bowl. Make a well in the centre and add the beaten eggs and the cooled fruit mixture. Mix quickly and well, then turn into a greased and lined tin. Either a 23 cm/9" round tin or a 900 g/2 lb loaf tin will do.

Bake at 160°C/325°F/gas 3 for 1½–2 hours.

Sultanas are dried green grapes and are usually larger and juicier than raisins.

AUNT MOLLIE'S SIMPLE FRUITCAKE

Aunt Mollie learned to cook late in life. Like many late-bloomers, she became most enthusiastic and pressed her recipes on all her friends and relations. This cake was popular with all of them and is quick to prepare. It can be made with any mixture of fruit and will keep fresh for several days in an airtight tin.

- 225 g/8 oz/2 cups white (all-purpose) flour
- 225 g/8 oz/1¾ cups dried fruit
- 75 g/3 oz/3 US tbsp sugar
- 1 tsp/1¼ US tsp mixed spice
- 1 tsp/1¼ US tsp cinnamon
- 75 g/3 oz/6 US tbsp margarine and butter, mixed
- 1 tbsp/1¼ US tbsp golden (Karo) syrup
- 175 ml/6 oz/¾ cup milk
- 1 tsp/generous 1 US tsp baking powder

Mix the flour, dried fruit, sugar and spices in a bowl. Melt the margarine, butter and golden/Karo syrup in a saucepan. Pour into flour mixture and mix well. Add milk and mix again. Add the baking powder and fold in gently.

Bake in a 450 g/1 lb loaf tin at 180°C/350°F/gas 4 for 1 hour and 20 minutes. Cool in the tin and put on a wire rack.

CHRISTMAS CAKE

Everyone has a special recipe for Christmas cake. Every December we are flooded with new ideas in nearly every newspaper. This recipe, from County Longford, has never been known to fail. This excellent cake will keep for many weeks.

- 225 g/8 oz/2 sticks butter
- 225 g/8 oz/1 cup sugar
- 450 g/1 lb/4 cups white (all-purpose) flour
- 6 large eggs, beaten
- 450 g/1 lb/3 cups sultanas*
- 225 g/8 oz/1¼ cups raisins
- 225 g/8 oz/1⅓ cups currants
- 125 g/4 oz/⅔ cup chopped mixed peel
- 50 g/2 oz/½ cup glacé cherries
- 1 level tsp/1¼ US tsp baking powder

Cream the butter and sugar together in a large bowl. Add the flour and beaten egg alternately, beating well after each addition. Add the dried fruit and mix well. Lastly, add the baking powder and mix thoroughly.

Bake in a 22 cm/9″ cake tin at 150°C/300°F/gas 2 for at least 2½ hours.

*Sultanas are dried green grapes and are usually larger and juicier than raisins.

Savoury and Sweet Pies

Rich Shortcrust Pastry

SAVOURY
Donegal Pie
Dingle Pie
Pork Pie
Steak and Kidney Pie with Guinness
Chicken Pie with Potato Pastry

SWEET
Traditional Apple Pie
Mince Pies
Gooseberry Lattice Tart

Meat pies may well have started in the Middle Ages. Medieval cooks wrapped meat in a flour and water paste to keep it moist when cooking. The paste, when taken off, was found to taste delightfully of meat and gravy.

Traditional meat pies consisted of plenty of meat and gravy in a deep dish, with a decorated crust of pastry covering the meat. The next step was to make fruit pies. These were made with slightly sweetened pastry and became Sunday treats in many Irish households.

Meat pies were usually eaten hot, except for those made with a hot water crust like pork pie. These became solid when cold and were used for picnics and other outdoor activities.

In Ireland, cooks sometimes mixed potato with the flour to make pies, as in the recipe on page 73. This was moistened with beaten egg. Shortcrust pastry, so often just moistened with water, was much richer with at least one egg yolk added, two yolks if more than 225 g/8 oz/2 cups of flour are used.

A floured rolling pin is a must for pastry-making, as well as a floured board. Deep, flat-edged pie dishes are hard to find but casserole dishes will do. There are plenty of tart plates on sale for flat tarts. Pork pie can be baked in a cake tin or, if it will hold together, on a baking sheet.

RICH SHORTCRUST PASTRY

The recipes in this section, whether sweet or savoury, use rich shortcrust pastry. Rich shortcrust pastry for sweet dishes such as gooseberry tart and mince pies needs 50 g/ 2 oz/2 US tbsp caster (superfine) sugar mixed into the pastry before the egg yolks are added. Otherwise, the pastry is the same.

- 275 g/10 oz/2½ cups white (all-purpose) flour
- 175 g/6 oz/1½ sticks butter or margarine, or a mixture
- pinch of salt
- 2 egg yolks
- a little water

Cut the butter and/or margarine into small pieces and mix it into the flour and salt with a knife. Then rub it with the fingertips to make it like breadcrumbs. Beat the egg yolks and add them to the mixture, extending them with a little very cold water to make a soft dough. This should not be wet but should leave the sides of the bowl clean. The dough should be flexible. Place the dough on a well-floured board and knead it lightly with floury hands for a minute or so. Roll it out very gently with a floured rolling pin, giving it a half turn every now and then to prevent it from sticking to the board. The pastry is now ready for use.

Savoury

DONEGAL PIE

A hearty savoury pie which is better cold than hot and wonderful for picnics in the rough weather of north-west Ireland. This is the pie to make in an emergency, as most people usually have all these ingredients in the house.

THE PASTRY

- 225 g/8 oz/2 cups white (all-purpose) flour
- 150 g/5 oz/1¼ sticks margarine or butter
- 1 egg yolk
- a little water

THE FILLING

- 450 g/1 lb potatoes
- chives and parsley, 1 dsp/2 US tbsp each
- salt to taste
- 3 hard-boiled eggs, sliced
- 4 fried rashers/slices of bacon

Make the rich shortcrust pastry (see Method, opposite). Set the dough aside while you make the filling. Steam, then mash the potatoes thoroughly. Mix in the herbs and salt to taste. Line the base of a pie plate with half of the potato-herb mixture. Spread a layer of hard-boiled egg over the potato. Cut the fried rashers/slices of bacon into small pieces and strew onto the sliced egg. Pour any bacon fat you have over this. Spread another layer of potatoes over the bacon. Roll out the pastry. Cover the filling with the pastry and bake at 200°C/400°F/gas 6 for 25–30 minutes. (If there is any extra pastry, add a pretty design to the top.) It is important to prevent the crust from becoming too dry. A covering of tin foil over the pie after the first 10 minutes helps with this.

DINGLE PIE

This tastes rather like a Cornish pastie and is a good picnic pie. Finely-chopped onion and carrot can be added to the meat mixture.

THE PASTRY
- 350 g/12 oz/3 cups white (all-purpose) flour
- 25 g/1 oz/¼ stick butter or margarine
- 2 egg yolks
- a little water

THE FILLING
- 350 g/12 oz lamb, cut in small pieces and trimmed
- salt
- pepper
- marjoram and chives, 1 dsp/2 US tbsp each
- stock or water to moisten

Make the rich shortcrust pastry (see Method, pages 66–7). Divide the dough — one piece should be slightly larger than the other. Roll out the larger piece to 20 cm/8″ in diameter and place on a pie plate. Arrange the meat on the pastry. Season it and sprinkle with chopped herbs. Moisten it with stock. Roll out the smaller piece of dough and place it over the top of the meat. Wet the pastry edges to fix them together. Press down with a fork. Brush the pie with the remains of the egg yolk mixed with a little milk. Bake at 200°C/400°F/gas 6 for 20 minutes. Then protect the pastry with tin foil and reduce the heat to finish cooking the meat, about 45 minutes.

PORK PIE

A satisfying picnic pie for outdoor people. The Irish version includes rashers/slices of bacon. This pie sometimes needs to be made a few times before the result is perfect!

THE FILLING

- 450 g/1 lb pork, diced in cubes
- 4 rashers/slices of bacon, chopped
- 1 tbsp/1¼ US tbsp each chives and thyme
- pepper

THE PASTRY

- 450 g/1 lb/4 cups white (all-purpose) flour
- 1 tsp/1¼ US tsp salt
- 215 ml/7½ oz/⅔ cup milk and water, ½ of each
- 200 g/7 oz/1 cup lard
- milk for glaze
- stock

Mix the pork, bacon and herbs in a small bowl. Sprinkle with pepper. Put the flour and salt into a warm mixing bowl. Heat the milk-water mixture with the lard until it is boiling. Pour it into a well in the centre of the flour mixture. Stir this with a wooden spoon and make it into a dough with your hands. Cut off ¼ of the dough and reserve. Keep it warm, covered with a clean towel, while you make a dough parcel for the filling.

Pat the dough into a thick, round piece. Place on a baking sheet. Put a round (900 g/2 lb) jam jar in the middle and start working the dough up the sides of the jar. Pull out the jar carefully when the dough is cool. The dough will 'relax' a bit and leave a hollow. Place the meat mixture inside the dough parcel and cover it with the rolled-out top made with the remaining dough. Make a hole in the middle of the top and brush the surface with milk.

Bake at 150°C/300°F/gas 2 for 1½ hours, covering with tin foil if the top is becoming too brown. Allow the pie to get cold before pouring in the stock. For jellied stock, cook pork or chicken bones separately.

STEAK AND KIDNEY PIE WITH GUINNESS

Guinness is sometimes used when braising beef and gives this traditional pie a rich but subtle flavour. Red wine is a good substitute if Guinness is not available.

THE FILLING

- 675 g/1½ lb steak ⎫
- 225 g/8 oz beef kidneys ⎬ cut up and trimmed
- flour to coat
- salt
- pepper
- 2 tbsp/2½ US tbsp each chopped thyme and marjoram
- 125 ml/4 oz/½ cup Guinness

THE PASTRY

- 275 g/10 oz/2½ cups white (all-purpose) flour
- 175 g/6 oz/1½ sticks butter or margarine
- 2 egg yolks
- a little water
- stock

Coat the steak and beef kidneys lightly with flour and arrange in a pie dish. Sprinkle with salt, pepper and herbs. Pour the Guinness over this. Set aside while you make the pastry (see Method, pages 66–7).

Cover the meat with the rolled-out pastry using an upturned egg cup to help support the pastry. Decorate the pie with leaves and brush it with the remains of the egg yolk.

Bake at 200°C/400°F/gas 6 for 15–20 minutes. Then reduce the heat to cook the meat more gently. This will take about 2 hours.

Put a dampened piece of tin foil firmly round the top of the pie to prevent the pastry from getting dry and to help lower the baking temperature. Test the meat with a skewer. Add a little hot stock to the pie just before serving.

CHICKEN PIE WITH POTATO PASTRY

The soft, old-fashioned potato pastry is well suited to the mildly savoury flavour of chicken. Rabbit may be used instead of chicken.

THE FILLING

- 1 chicken, boned and cut in pieces (use the bones for stock)
- flour to dredge
- oil and butter to fry
- 3 tomatoes, skinned and chopped
- chives and parsley, chopped
- 4 tbsp/5 US tbsp Smithwicks (dark) beer or lemon juice
- 4 rashers (slices) of lean bacon, cut in strips

Flour the chicken pieces and fry them in a mixture of oil and butter until they are golden brown. Place them in a shallow casserole dish. Scatter the chopped tomato and herbs over the chicken and pour over the beer. Cover this with a layer of bacon rashers/slices.

THE PASTRY

- 150 g/5 oz/1¼ cups self-raising white flour
- 125 g/4 oz/1 stick butter or margarine
- 75 g/3 oz/about ½ cup mashed potato
- pinch of salt
- 1 egg, beaten

Rub the butter into the flour. Add the mashed potato and salt and mix well. Add the beaten egg. Knead this on a floured board until it is soft and elastic. Roll it out to 1¾ cm/⅜″ and place it on top of the bacon rashers. Make leaves to decorate and brush with melted butter. Bake at 200°C/400°F/gas 6 for 20 minutes. Then reduce the heat until the chicken is cooked, about 30 minutes.

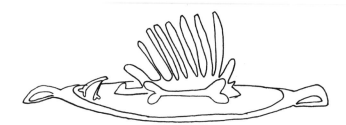

Sweet

TRADITIONAL APPLE PIE

Strictly speaking, apple pie needs an old-fashioned pie dish with a flat edge. It can, however, be made in a casserole dish just as well. Apple pie is made more interesting by slipping in two or three plums, a handful of blackberries or one or two cloves.

THE PASTRY

■ 225 g/8 oz/2 cups white (all-purpose) flour

■ 150 g/5 oz/1¼ sticks butter or margarine

■ 50 g/2 oz/¼ cup caster (superfine) sugar

■ 1 egg yolk

■ a little cold water

THE FILLING

■ 900 g/2 lb apples, sliced

■ 125 g/4 oz/½ cup brown sugar

■ 125 ml/4 oz/½ cup orange juice or water

■ caster (superfine) sugar for sprinkling

Make the rich shortcrust pastry with added sugar (see Method, pages 66–7). Leave the dough while you make the filling. Slice the apples and place them in a small pie dish with the brown sugar and orange juice or water. Put an up-turned egg cup in the dish to hold up the pastry.

Roll out the pastry to 2½ cm/1" larger than your chosen pie dish. Slide it over the apples or roll it round a floured rolling pin and roll back over the dish. Prick the edges attractively. Brush the top with milk.

Bake at 200°C/400°F/gas 6 for 15 minutes. Then reduce the heat or put the pie lower in the oven for another 30 minutes. Sprinkle the pie with caster (superfine) sugar before serving.

MINCE PIES

A classic recipe, particularly at Christmas. In Ireland, mince pies are usually little individual tartlets rather than the large pies which Americans are used to.

THE PASTRY

- 275 g/10 oz/2½ cups white (all-purpose) flour
- 200 g/7 oz/1¾ sticks butter
- 50 g/2 oz/2 US tbsp caster (superfine) sugar
- 2 egg yolks, beaten
- a little water
- caster (superfine) sugar for sprinkling

THE FILLING

- 675 g/1½ lb/2½ cups (approximately) mincemeat
- 2 tbsp/2½ US tbsp whiskey

Mix the mincemeat and whiskey in a small bowl. Make the pastry (see Method, pages 66–7). Divide the pastry in two. Roll out half of the pastry thinly. Stamp out rounds to fit a patty/muffin tin. Roll out the other half of the pastry. Stamp the rounds on this half a little larger.

Arrange the pastry from the second rolling in the patty/muffin tins. Put in a generous spoonful of mincemeat. Cover with the smaller pastry rounds, wetting the edges and pressing down with a fork. Glaze with the remains of egg yolk, mixed with a little milk. Bake at 200°C/400°F/gas 6 for about 20 minutes.

Sprinkle caster (superfine) sugar over the pies as soon as they come out of the oven. Put them on a wire rack when cool. Serve with brandy butter, whiskey butter or cream. Brandy and whiskey butter are made by mixing softened butter with icing/confectioners' sugar or caster (superfine) sugar and brandy or whiskey.

GOOSEBERRY LATTICE TART

Gooseberries are ripe in June in Ireland. The lattice tart looks attractive. It is substantial and tangy and tastes best hot but is also good cold.

THE PASTRY

- 400 g/14 oz/3½ cups white flour
- 225 g/8 oz/2 sticks margarine or butter
- 50 g/2 oz/2 US tbsp caster (superfine) sugar
- 2 egg yolks
- a little water
- milk to glaze

THE FILLING

- 450 g/1 lb gooseberries
- 125 g/4 oz/½ cup demerara (granulated brown) sugar

Top and tail the gooseberries and set aside. Make the rich sweetened shortcrust pastry (see Method, pages 66–7) and set the dough aside. Cut off ¼ of the dough and reserve for the lattice. Roll out the larger piece of dough and place on a flan/pie dish. Let the edges of pastry come 2½ cm/1" over the sides. Then turn them back, wet them and pinch together.

Empty the gooseberries over the pastry and sprinkle with demerara (granulated brown) sugar. Roll out the reserved dough and cut it into strips. Arrange these in a lattice pattern over the gooseberries. Brush the top of the pastry with egg yolk mixed with a little milk.

Bake at 200°C/400°F/gas 6 for 20 minutes to set the pastry and brown it a little. Then reduce the heat to 190°C/375°F/gas 5. Cover the top with damp tin foil to cook the gooseberries, about 45 minutes. Keep warm. Before serving, sprinkle with caster (superfine) sugar.

Puddings

Apple Charlotte
Friar's Omelette
Fruit Crumble
Baked Carrot Pudding
Rhubarb Sponge
Summer Shortcake
Blackberry Crunch
October Cobbler

In the old days, the air inside Irish houses was often as cold and damp as the air outside. The warm sweetness of pudding was therefore most comforting, and cooks who had the time made puddings every day. These were usually steamed in a bowl in boiling water.

Since houses are now warmer, steamed puddings are made less often and their place has been taken by lighter baked puddings made with seasonal fruit.

The fruit rhythm of the Irish year is this. Six months of apples are followed in March and April by rhubarb. Rhubarb is tender until June, when the gooseberries are ripe. These are succeeded in July by red and black currants and rasp-berries. Then towards autumn come pears, plums, early apples and blackberries.

These recipes include all this fruit, accompanied by some kind of light flour mixture or breadcrumbs. The exception is the carrot pudding. The carrot is grated straight into the flour mixture, making the pudding pleasantly moist.

APPLE CHARLOTTE

There are at least three ways of making this traditional pudding, so popular with all ages. This one is the easiest. Because of the long cooking time, the apples, sugar, spices and butter take on a delicious toffee taste, with the bread merging in.

- 6 slices of white bread and butter, crusts removed
- 4 large cooking apples, cut into chunks
- 150 g/5 oz/⅔ cup demerara (granulated brown) sugar
- 1 tsp/1¼ US tsp each cinnamon and coriander
- juice of 1 orange

Cut the bread and butter into fingers. Line the bottom of a small, deep casserole with one-third of these. Cover with half of the apples. Sprinkle with half the sugar and half the spices. Pour half the orange juice over the surface. Repeat the whole process. Cover the top layer of apples with the remaining bread fingers. Sprinkle with the remaining sugar and spices.Fit a piece of tin foil over the top and bake at 180°C/350°F/gas 4 for 1½ hours, removing the tin foil for the last 20 minutes.

FRIAR'S OMELETTE

This light and unusual pudding is a variation of a recipe from 1804.

- 450 g/1 lb cooking apples, sliced
- 125 g/4 oz/½ cup brown sugar
- juice of ½ lemon
- cinnamon and coriander (optional)
- 25 g/1 oz/¼ stick butter
- 125 g/4 oz/2 cups fresh breadcrumbs
- 2 eggs, well beaten

Cook the sliced apples with 2 tbsp/2½ US tbsp water and all but 1½–2 tbsp of the brown sugar until they form a purée. Add the lemon juice, spices and butter. Allow this to get cold. Line a shallow baking casserole with about half the breadcrumbs. Beat the eggs into the cold apple mixture. Put this into the dish and cover with the remaining breadcrumbs. Bake at 180°C/350°F/gas 4 for 30 minutes. If it is not brown enough on top, put the pudding under a hot grill/broiler for a few minutes. Sprinkle with the remaining brown sugar and serve with cream.

FRUIT CRUMBLE

This is one of Ireland's best-known puddings and deserves to be. Quickly made, almost any fruit (or a mixture of fruits) will do for the filling, although apple is the most popular.

THE FILLING
- 450 g/1 lb fruit
- 125 g/4 oz/½ cup demerara (granulated brown) sugar
- juice of 1 orange

THE CRUMBLE
- 125 g/4 oz/1 cup white (all-purpose) flour
- 25 g/1 oz/¼ cup oatmeal
- 50 g/2 oz/½ stick butter
- 50 g/2 oz/¼ cup demerara (granulated brown) sugar
- grated rind of 1 orange
- 1 tsp ground coriander

Cut up and prepare the fruit and place it in a shallow baking dish. Sprinkle it with the demerara (granulated brown) sugar and squeeze over the orange juice. Rub the flour and oatmeal into the butter. When the mixture is like breadcrumbs, add the sugar, orange rind and coriander. Sprinkle the flour mixture over the fruit and bake at 200°C/400°F/gas 6 until the crumble is light brown and the fruit is soft, about 30 minutes. It is important not to have too thick a crumble as this can be stodgy. Fruit crumble can be kept warm for some time without suffering.

BAKED CARROT PUDDING

An excellent use for large carrots, this pudding is unexpectedly juicy and refreshing.

- 150 g/5 oz carrots, coarsely grated
- 125 g/4 oz/1 stick butter or margarine
- 125 g/4 oz/1 cup self-raising white flour
- 1 tsp cinnamon
- 1 tsp coriander
- 125 g/4 oz/½ cup demerara (granulated brown) sugar
- 50 g/2 oz/½ cup candied peel

Grate the carrots coarsely and set aside. Cream the butter or margarine. Put the flour and spices into a mixing bowl. Add the sugar. Mix the butter into the dry ingredients. Then add the grated carrot and candied peel, mixing all the time. Put the mixture into a baking dish and cook at 200°C/400°F/ gas 6 for approximately 1 hour. You may need to cover the dish with tin foil to prevent dryness. The grated carrot will keep the pudding moist and sweet. Serve directly from the baking dish and pour cream over each individual serving.

RHUBARB SPONGE

Made in late spring, this tangy sponge takes advantage of the seasonal surplus of rhubarb. A similar sponge made with stewed apple is called Eve's Pudding. This old favourite can also be made with stewed plums or gooseberries.

- 350 g/¾ lb rhubarb
- 125 g/4 oz/½ cup brown sugar
- juice of 1 orange
- 65 g/2½ oz/½ stick margarine or butter
- 65 g/2½ oz/2½ US tbsp white sugar
- 150 g/5 oz/1¼ cups self-raising white flour
- 1 egg, beaten
- 2 tbsp/2½ US tbsp milk (approximately)

Cut up the rhubarb and put in a flattish casserole dish. Sprinkle with the brown sugar. Squeeze the orange juice over this and put the dish in the oven to stew, covered with tin foil. After 20 minutes, or when fruit is cooked, remove from the oven and cool a little.

Meanwhile, cream the margarine or butter and sugar. Add the flour and beaten egg alternately. Add the milk carefully and mix well. Spread this mixture carefully on top of the fruit.

Bake at 200°C/400°F/ gas 6, putting tin foil over if it threatens to burn. Cooking time is 30–40 minutes. Serve with thick cream.

SUMMER SHORTCAKE

Half-way between a cake and a pudding, this has a sweet but sharp taste. It is very quickly made as, unlike most shortcakes, it includes beaten egg. Use only 1 oz/1 US tablespoon of sugar on the fruit or it will become jam. This shortcake is also good in the autumn using blackberries and pears.

- 175 g/6 oz/1½ cups self-raising white flour
- 90 g/3½ oz/⅔ stick butter or margarine
- 75 g/3 oz/3 US tbsp sugar
- 1 egg, beaten
- 400 g/14 oz/2 cups raspberries
- 50 g/2 oz/⅓ cup red or white currants

Rub the butter into the flour. Add 50 g/2 oz/2 US tbsp sugar. Add the beaten egg. Mix well, then knead until a soft dough is formed. Roll out to 1¼ cm/½". Put the raspberries and currants into a baking dish with the remaining sugar. Place the dough on top. Brush it with egg or milk.

Bake for 20 minutes at 200°C/400°F/gas 6. It should become an attractive golden colour. Sprinkle with caster (superfine) sugar and serve with cream.

BLACKBERRY CRUNCH

Blackberries are especially large and delicious in the rainy West of Ireland. There, they are ripe in late August. In the rest of the country, they ripen later. Pears go well with blackberries and are in season at the same time. They can be included in this country pudding.

- 450 g/1 lb blackberries
- 5 tbsp/6½ US tbsp caster (superfine) sugar
- 50 g/2 oz/1 cup brown breadcrumbs
- 125 g/4 oz/⅔ cup icing (confectioners') sugar
- 1 tsp/1¼ US tsp cinnamon
- 75 g/3 oz/¾ stick melted butter or margarine

Mix the blackberries and caster (superfine) sugar in a small pie dish or casserole and leave the sugar to soak in. Mix the breadcrumbs, icing/confectioners' sugar and cinnamon. Add the melted butter. Cover the blackberries with this mixture. Bake at 200°C/400°F/gas 6 for 30 minutes.

OCTOBER COBBLER

A seasonal pudding using your favourite autumn fruit.

- 450 g/1 lb autumn fruit mixture — blackberries, apples, pears, plums, damsons, elderberries (if possible some dark fruit)
- 3 tbsp/4 US tbsp sugar
- 1 tbsp/1¼ US tbsp lemon juice
- 150 g/5 oz/1¼ stick butter
- 175 g/6 oz/1½ cups self-raising white flour

- 25 g/1 oz/1 US tbsp caster (superfine) sugar
- 3 tbsp/4 US tbsp milk

Clean the fruit and cut it up if necessary. Put fruit in a casserole dish. Cover with sugar and squeeze over the lemon juice. Dot with 25 g/1 oz/¼ stick of the butter.

Rub the remaining butter into the flour. Add the caster (superfine) sugar and mix in the milk until the sides of the bowl are clean. Quickly make an elastic dough. Roll it out carefully to about 1¼ cm/½" and place over the fruit. Tidy the edges and prick the pastry well.

Brush with milk and bake at 200°C/400°F/gas 6 for about 40 minutes, or until golden brown. Sprinkle the cobbler with caster (superfine) sugar and serve with cream.

Baking Without Flour

SAVOURY
Stuffed Vegetables
Liver and Bacon with Guinness
Scallops
Family Salmon Pie
Tomato Monkfish Bake

SWEET
Sliced and Spiced Apples
Whole Apples with Irish Whiskey
Pears with Cashel Blue Cheese
Baked Pears with Irish Mist

Sometimes Ireland's excellent fish, meat and fruit can be baked deliciously without any accompanying pastry or flour mixture. Baking emphasises flavours and concentrates nourishment. Baked dishes are also easy to bring to the table. If accompanied by salad and homemade bread, in the case of savoury dishes, there need be no fluster with pots and pans. Sweet bakes can be served with shortbread biscuits.

The recipes include three fish dishes. Fish is so fresh and so varied in Ireland and known to be so good for our health. All you need for baking fish is a spoonful or two of cream or milk, a few slivers of butter, a dusting of Parmesan cheese and browned breadcrumbs. Another recipe, liver baked and covered with bacon rashers (page 90), keeps its moisture and flavour far better than fried liver.

Apples can be insipid. Spiced with Irish whiskey and covered with sultanas and demerara (granulated brown) sugar, they take on a new and interesting flavour. Pears are made more tangy when contrasted with Cashel blue cheese or with Irish Mist liqueur.

Savoury
STUFFED VEGETABLES

Beefsteak tomatoes and small marrows are the best for this attractive dish. True marrows are hard to buy now that the shops are flooded with skinny courgettes. It is worth trying to grow marrows, and not difficult. They are best cut at about one-third their final size when they still have a delicate flavour but will also provide enough hollow for stuffing.

- 2 beefsteak tomatoes
- 1 small marrow
- 450 g/1 lb freshly-minced (ground) steak
- chopped thyme and chives
- salt and pepper
- 4 rashers (slices) of bacon, cut in strips

Halve the tomatoes and scoop the pulp into a bowl, throwing out the core. Cut the marrow in half from top to bottom and scoop out the seeds. Cut into a few large pieces and boil for 10 minutes. Drain them. Mix the minced/ground meat into the pulped tomatoes and add the salt, pepper and herbs. Fill the tomato halves and the hollow pieces of marrow with the mixture. Scatter the tops with strips of bacon.

Place everything in a large, flat baking dish, handsome enough to bring to the table. Bake the stuffed tomato and marrow at 200°C/400°F/ gas 6 until the meat is cooked, the marrow tender and the bacon crisp.

A spicy variation of this is to fill scooped marrow with soft breadcrumbs, herbs and bacon rashers/slices already chopped and fried. Vegetarians will omit the bacon, adding diced mushrooms or extra breadcrumbs.

LIVER AND BACON WITH GUINNESS

Liver is far more succulent cooked this way than when it is grilled or fried. Guinness makes a delicately-flavoured gravy. Sliced mushrooms or skinned tomatoes can be included in this nourishing dish. Any green vegetable in season can accompany it.

- 2 slices white bread
- 1 dsp/2 US tbsp (all-purpose) flour
- 450 g/1 lb liver, sliced, trimmed and blanched
- chives, parsley or thyme
- 6 thinly-cut rashers (slices) of bacon
- 4 tbsp/5 US tbsp Guinness
- 2 tbsp/2½ US tbsp water

Cut the bread in thin slices and spread these on the bottom of a shallow casserole. Place the liver slices over the bread and dredge the flour over the liver. Sprinkle on the herbs. Cover everything with the bacon. Pour in the Guinness and the water to make a gravy.

Bake at 190–200°C/375–400°F/gas 5–6 until the bacon is crisp, about 35 minutes. A juicy, delicious gravy should have formed naturally, and the bread should be well absorbed. Serve at once.

SCALLOPS

The Irish have been revelling in seafood of late, and scallops are plentiful in coastal areas. This is a simple way of cooking them. Other seafood can be added to this dish. Instead of wine, you can use a little milk or cream.

- 8 king scallops
- salt and pepper
- 1 tbsp/1¼ tbsp each chopped chives and parsley
- 2 or 3 tbsp/2¼–4 US tbsp dry white wine or lemon juice
- brown breadcrumbs
- butter

Cut the scallops in half. Sprinkle them with salt and pepper and arrange in a shallow casserole dish. Sprinkle over the herbs. Spoon the white wine or lemon juice over the scallops. Sprinkle them thinly with brown breadcrumbs and arrange slivers of butter over them. Bake at 190°C/375°F/gas 5 until the fish is cooked. Serve at once.

FAMILY SALMON PIE

Irish salmon is famous, wild or farmed, and easy to come by. This economical way to use up left-over salmon is popular in many families.

- 900 g/2 lb mature potatoes
- 75 g/3 oz/¾ stick butter
- 280 ml/½ pint/1¼ cups hot milk, approximately
- salt and pepper
- 225 g/8 oz/1 cup cooked salmon, flaked

Boil or steam the potatoes and mash them. Keep them hot and beat in 50 g/2 oz/½ stick butter and enough hot milk to make the potatoes a dropping consistency — almost liquid. Add salt and pepper and taste the mixture for seasoning.

Put a layer of the potato mixture in the bottom of a shallow casserole. Spread the flaked salmon over this, then add the rest of the potato, criss-crossing the top with a fork. Take the remaining butter and cut into slivers over the top of the pie.

Bake at 200°C/400°F/gas 6 until bubbling and golden brown. Finish the top under the grill/broiler if necessary.

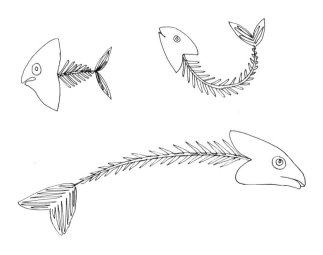

TOMATO MONKFISH BAKE

Monkfish produces a delicious sauce when cooked this way. It is essential not to use too many tomatoes, as they can obliterate the delicate taste. Other white fish are suitable for this dish, but monkfish is firm and solid and tastes the best.

- 450 g/1 lb monkfish, skinned and boned
- 2 tbsp/2½ US tbsp marjoram and thyme, chopped
- salt and pepper
- 3 tomatoes, skinned and chopped
- 2 tbsp/2½ US tbsp cream

Cut the fish into bite-size pieces and place in a shallow casserole. Sprinkle with half the herbs. Add salt and pepper. Top with the chopped tomato. Cover with tin foil and bake at 180°C/350°F/gas 4 until the fish is cooked, about 20 minutes. Pour over the cream and sprinkle with the remaining herbs. Serve immediately with new potatoes and mange tout/sugar snap peas.

Sweet
SLICED AND SPICED APPLES

These are refreshing when served after a robust stew or roast.

- 3 large cooking apples
- 175 g/6 oz/⅔ cup demerara (granulated brown) sugar
- 50 g/2 oz/½ cup candied peel
- 3 tbsp/4 US tbsp Irish whiskey
- 50 g/2 oz/½ stick butter

Slice the apples very thinly. Arrange a layer of them in a shallow casserole dish. Sprinkle on some sugar and candied peel. Carry on filling the casserole with layers of fruit and sprinkles of sugar and peel. Before the last layer of sugar, pour over the whiskey. Finish with a thick layer of sugar. Cut slivers of butter to scatter over the sugar. Cover with tin foil and bake at 200°C/400°F/gas 6 for about 35 minutes. If you want the top to be browner, take off the tin foil for the last 10 minutes. Serve with cream.

WHOLE APPLES WITH IRISH WHISKEY

Baked apples, usually so dull and dreary, have an exotic flavour cooked this way. There are many variations of this recipe. Try stuffing the apples with candied peel and pouring red wine over them.

- 4 large cooking apples
- 3 dsp/5 US tbsp sultanas (dried green grapes)
- 3 tbsp/4 US tbsp Irish whiskey
- 4 dsp/6 US tbsp demerara (granulated brown) sugar
- 1 tsp/1¼ US tsp cinnamon
- 50 g/2 oz/½ stick butter
- a little water

Steep the sultanas in the whiskey for 2 hours before you start cooking. Put 2 or 3 tablespoons of water in a shallow casserole. Core the apples, cut round their equator and arrange them in the dish. Drain the sultanas and pack them into the apple centres, setting the whiskey aside. Fill up the centres with sugar and cinnamon. Spoon over the whiskey and place slivers of butter on the apples.

Bake at 200°C/400°F/gas 6 for about 35 minutes or until the apples are completely soft. They can be tested with a carving fork. Baste them occasionally. Serve at once with cream and brown sugar.

PEARS WITH CASHEL BLUE CHEESE

Cashel Blue cheese is produced from the milk of a pedi-gree Friesian herd, grazing on lush Tipperary pastures. Other spicy baked dishes can be made using this strong but creamy cheese. The sharp taste of the cheese contrasts well with the sweetness of dessert pears. Use more cheese if you like a more pungent flavour.

- 4 dessert pears, halved
- 50 g/2 oz/½ cup Cashel Blue cheese
- 25 g/1 oz/¼ stick butter, melted
- 50 g/2 oz/2 US tbsp demerara (granulated brown) sugar

Take a thin slice off the round side of 4 pear halves (to make them lie steadily on the dish). Place these halves on a shallow casserole dish. Cut the cheese into thin slices and place these on top of the pear halves. Arrange the remaining pear halves on top, round side up, to make a pear sandwich. Pour melted butter over the pears and sprinkle with the demerara (granulated brown) sugar, adding 2 tbsp/2½ US tbsp water to prevent burning.

Bake at 200°C/400°F/gas 6 until the pears are golden brown and soft and the cheese has started to melt. Serve at once, handing round more sugar to sprinkle on top.

BAKED PEARS WITH IRISH MIST

Best made with dessert pears. The sauce generates itself and becomes sweet but tangy. If you find this too bland, use more liqueur.

- 4 dessert pears
- 25 g/1 oz/¼ stick butter
- 75 g/3 oz/3 US tbsp demerara (granulated brown) sugar
- juice of 1 orange
- 2 tbsp/2½ US tbsp Irish Mist liqueur
- 2 tbsp/2½ US tbsp cream

Peel, core and halve the pears. Place them flat side down in a shallow casserole dish. Melt the butter and sugar in the orange juice over a very low heat. Add the Irish Mist. Pour this over the pears and bake them at 200°C/400°F/gas 6 for 20–25 minutes, basting the pears with the liquid and turning them over once or twice. Take them out of the oven, pour over the cream and serve at once.

Index